MW00876690

IN MY
Father's
GARDEN

By Michael Freiling

PRESS

Copyright © 2002 by Michael Freiling

In My Father's Garden
by Michael Freiling

Printed in the United States of America

Library of Congress Control Number: 2002113895
ISBN 1-591603-39-0

All rights reserved. No part of this publication may be reproduced or transmitted in any form or by any means without written permission of the publisher.

Xulon Press
11350 Random Hills Road
Suite 800
Fairfax, VA 22030
(703) 279-6511
XulonPress.com

To order additional copies, call 1-866-909-BOOK (2665).

Dedicated to
our three sons:

Tom

Bob

John

Table of Contents

Introduction

This book started as my hobby, with a backyard garden full of plants and flowers that had Christian names.

My wife's love of the Lord and almost continuous Bible reading made the search for the verses, scriptures, and passages a real pleasure.

The time spent looking through catalogues of daylily plants and the hours of great Bible reading gave us many hours of enjoyment.

Now, our backyard is in bloom with a variety of wonderful daylilies of many different sizes, colors, and fragrances, and our hearts are full of wonderful scriptures, each special to us and to each individual flower.

We hope that you will enjoy the pictures, scriptures, and descriptions as much as we enjoyed creating this book.

Daylily List

Temple of Heaven

This is, I believe, a vision of Armageddon where the angels will come from heaven for the final harvest. These angels will use their sickles to cut off the clusters of grapes (the evil) from the vines of the earth, for they will be fully ripe for judgment. This is the fulfillment of the wrath of God as revealed in Revelation:

> *Then an angel came from the temple and called to him, "Begin to use the sickle, for the time has come for you to reap; the harvest is ripe on the earth." So the one sitting on the cloud swung his sickle over the earth, and the harvest was gathered in. After that another angel came from the temple in heaven, and he also had a sharp sickle.*
> *(Revelation 14:15–17 TLB)*

This is 33 inches tall and is beautiful pure pink with a deep green throat and upper gold coloring. It has darker pink pie-crusted petal edges and overlapping petals. Its four-inch flowers have perfect form.

Jude

Jude wrote his epistle about A.D. 68. His theme was "contending for the faith." Jude was one of the brothers of the Lord Jesus. His message was one of the most severe in the New Testament and warned and urged his readers to contend for the faith.

> **Jude, the servant of Jesus Christ, and brother of James, to them that are sanctified by God the Father, and preserved in Jesus Christ, and called.**
>
> ***(Jude 1 KJV)***

Jude is a smaller plant that usually grows to about 17 inches in height. It has a five- to six-inch flower that is an ivory-pink blend with a green throat. It's an extended bloomer, giving many hours of flowers to enjoy.

Damascus Road

The book of Acts tells the exciting account of Paul's conversion. Remember that he set out to destroy every Christian. As he was on his way to Damascus, the Lord suddenly came to him and struck him blind. For three days he stayed that way; however, the Lord knew that some day Paul would take his message to all nations. Let's review Acts 9 for that great change in him:

> *So Ananias went over and found Paul and laid his hands on him and said, "Brother Paul, the Lord Jesus, who appeared to you on the road, has sent me so that you may be filled with the Holy Spirit and get your sight back."*
>
> *(Acts 9:17 TLB)*

This is a beautiful burgundy flower measuring four to five inches. This looks just great with the light pink "Temple of Heaven." Add a white plant such as "Glory Glory," and it's a real garden treat.

Demetrius

Demetrius of 3 John was a man who was well respected. He was a believer of lofty reputation because he lived in the truth. In fact, the theme of 3 John is "walking in truth." Let's see what the apostle John wrote about him in his letter to his friend Gaius:

> ***Demetrius is well spoken of by everyone—and even by the truth itself. We also speak well of him, and you know that our testimony is true.***
> ***(3 John 12 NIV)***

This is another beautiful chrome-yellow flower with a five- to six-inch blossom. It grows to be 24 inches tall and will look great in any garden.

Bathsheba

You know the story of Bathsheba and David. In David's quest to marry Bathsheba, he had her husband (Uriah) sent to the front lines in the war. So the Lord sent the prophet Nathan to tell David a story about wrongdoing. David then confessed his sin and was forgiven, but because of his sin lost their first child.

> *Then Bathsheba bowed low with her face to the ground and, kneeling before the king, said, "May my lord King David live forever!"*
>
> *(1 Kings 1:31 NIV)*

Lifted Praise

Did the Lord lift his hands in praise? In Psalm 118, we can find verses that magnify the great joy and victory that can be expressed in giving thanks to the Lord. Let's read this wonderful section of the Bible:

The Lord's right hand has done mighty things!
The Lord's right hand is lifted high; the Lord's right
hand has done mighty things!
(Psalm 118:15–16 NIV)

This is one of those wonderful daylilies that seem to change color in the evening. It is also a repeat bloomer, making it an even more attractive flower for your garden. It is a very ruffled, creped, glittering light golden peach with a colored raised rib. The wide yellow throat blends almost halfway up the petals. In the evening the rib is pink! The other colors are lighter. It's a must for your garden. These repeat bloomers are almost like having two plants instead of one. You ought to put this plant next to "Lifted Hands" in your garden and have the double joy of two plants that change colors in the evening.

On to Glory

"Glory" is mentioned 295 times in the Bible. In reading the verses that mention "glory," the one that best describes the plant "On to Glory" is found in Hebrews. The theme of Hebrews is the priesthood of Christ. The second chapter teaches that Jesus was made like his brothers. Let's read the verses that best identify with "On to Glory":

In bringing many sons to glory, it was fitting that God, for whom and through whom everything exists, should make the author of their salvation perfect through suffering. Both the one who makes men holy and those who are made holy are of the same family. So Jesus is not ashamed to call them brothers.
(Hebrews 2:10–11 NIV)

Just as you would expect, this flower is the color of gold—just as our home in Glory will be. Can't you see the angels working in the gardens of heaven right now? This flower is lightly creped, very ruffled butter yellow with gold veining, light yellow shading, a flat rib, yellow-green throat, and green heart. It has a lot of gold on the sepals. As an extra treat, this is another beautiful repeat bloomer. It is a must for your garden. It would look great next to the diamond-dusted "Glory Glory" daylily!

Heavenly Aura

If you look up the word "aura" in the dictionary, it will say the following: "1: a distinctive atmosphere surrounding a given source, 2: a luminous radiation." To me, this description sounds like one that would match what we'll see heaven. As I searched the Bible for a verse to use for this daylily, I came across the perfect one. I found it in Deuteronomy in the fourth chapter, where idolatry was described and taught against. Let's read this verse:

And when you look up to the sky and see the sun, the moon and the stars—all the heavenly array—do not be enticed into bowing down to them and worshiping things the Lord your God has apportioned to all the nations under heaven.
(Deuteronomy 4:19 NIV)

This is one of those wonderful lavender-colored flowers that were in your grandmother's garden years ago. It is a tall, 35–inch plant with a 5–inch bloom. The lavender bloom is ruffled and has rose veining. The large yellow-green throat blends high up on its segments and ends in beautiful light maroon markings. In the evening the color is more of a light rose. A great flower. Try it with your favorite white daylily!

Heavenly Adobe

Again we had to go to the dictionary to see what "adobe" means. Well, it is brick that is used for building. The verse that relates to this is found in Genesis, where the story of the tower of Babel is told. Remember they wanted to make a tower that would reach heaven so that they would make a name for themselves and would not be scattered over the face of the earth. You know the rest of the story, don't you? Let's read that passage from the Bible:

> *They said to each other, "Come, let's make bricks and bake them thoroughly." They used brick instead of stone, and tar for mortar. Then they said, "Come, let us build ourselves a city, with a tower that reaches to the heavens, so that we may make a name for ourselves and not be scattered over the face of the whole earth."*
> *(Genesis 11:3–4 NIV)*

This is a superb flower with one of the most beautifully colored blossoms of all! Let's read about its colors. It is diamond-dusted, creped, fluffed light yellow with very delicate rose shading on the petal edges and airbrushed near the throat and on the sepals. It has a wide cream raised rib, wide triangular yellow throat, and green heart. In the morning, light rose shading is airbrushed over all of the petals and ends in a slight watermark at the end of the yellow-green throat. What a beauty! It is 24 inches tall with 6–inch blooms.

Elijah's Mantle

Second Kings tells of the ministry of Elisha. In that writing, which was written about the sixth century B.C., we see that Elisha received a double portion of Elijah's spirit. Let's read the verses that tell of the mantle of Elijah:

He took up also the mantle of Elijah that fell from him, and went back, and stood by the bank of Jordan; And he took the mantle of Elijah that fell from him, and smote the waters, and said, Where is the Lord God of Elijah? and when he also had smitten the waters, they parted hither and thither: and Elisha went over.

(2 Kings 2:13–14 KJV)

This is a beautiful fragrant flower with striking colors. It is rose red with slight medium burgundy shading at the edges. Its raised rib goes one-third of the way up the segments. It has a large strong yellow-green throat. By evening, the color is a lighter rose red. The plant is 32 inches tall with excellent branching.

Divine Word

What do you think would be an example of the Lord's divine Word? God's Word is so good that I had to look at many verses to select the one that I feel best represents the "Divine Word." Second Peter is the book I selected. Let's read it and see what I think is the divine Word:

> *His divine power has given us everything we need for life and godliness through our knowledge of him who called us by his own glory and goodness. Through these he has given us his very great and precious promises, so that through them you may participate in the divine nature and escape the corruption in the world caused by evil desires.*
> *(2 Peter 1:3–4 NIV)*

This flower is a tetraploid with great blossoms. It is a cream and pink combination that is in itself divine.

Angel Stuff

Well now, what kind of "stuff" are angels made out of anyway? It's strange that a flower can have such a simple name, and it's a challenge to find a verse in the Bible that would portray "Angel Stuff." But you know what? There is a verse that does just that. I found it in Hebrews, and it is as short and direct as needed:

> *To which of the angels did God ever say, "Sit at my right hand until I make your enemies a footstool for your feet"? Are not all angels ministering spirits sent to serve those who will inherit salvation?*
> *(Hebrews 1:13–14 NIV)*

Just like the beauty of an angel, this flower has a bloom that is brilliant yellow with a mahogany eye.

Moment of Truth

What do you think is a good verse for this flower? After searching the Word, I came into the part in Matthew that talks about the fulfillment of the Law. That, to me, is certainly the scripture that describes this plant, the "Moment of Truth." Let's read it now and see if you don't agree:

> *I tell you the truth, until heaven and earth disappear, not the smallest letter, not the least stroke of a pen, will by any means disappear from the Law until everything is accomplished. Anyone who breaks one of the least of these commandments and teaches others to do the same will be called least in the kingdom of heaven, but whoever practices and teaches these commands will be called great in the kingdom of heaven.*
>
> *(Matthew 5:18–19 NIV)*

When we talk about "truth," I think of purity. This flower is nearly white, just like truth is expressed to me. The plant is 23 inches tall and has a beautiful bloom of 6 inches. These white daylilies look so wonderful next to red, rose, or burgundy flowers. Mix some up for a real treat.

Trinity

The Holy Trinity—Father, Son, and Holy Spirit! I think it is best to use the scripture from Matthew that tells us about the baptism of Jesus. This was when Jesus saw the Spirit of God and he heard a voice from heaven saying, "This is my Son." This certainly is the verse of choice for describing the Trinity. Let's read that wonderful part of the gospel of Matthew:

> **As soon as Jesus was baptized, he went up out of the water. At that moment heaven was opened, and he saw the Spirit of God descending like a dove and lighting on him. And a voice from heaven said, "This is my Son, whom I love; with him I am well pleased."**
> **(Matthew 3:16–17 NIV)**

The flower "Trinity" is a blend of pinks. It's another beautiful flower with lots of blooms. It looks well in a garden with some reds and whites. This is a very nice daylily.

Highway to Heaven

What do you think—is there a reference to some kind of road to heaven in the Bible? Yes, there sure is. It's very plain that Jacob saw heaven in his dream. Remember Jacob's dream at Bethel? He fell asleep and had a vision of heaven. After he awoke, he made this vow:

> **Then Jacob made a vow, saying, "If God will be with me and will watch over me on this journey I am taking and will give me food to eat and clothes to wear so that I return safely to my father's house, then the Lord will be my God."**
>
> **(Genesis 28:20–21 NIV)**

This is a real beauty. Its colors are a nice blend of pale cream and light lavender pink with a chartreuse throat extending far out. The petals and sepals have light gold serrated edges. It has four-way branching.

Christmas Charm

This is a beautiful name and an equally beautiful flower. The verse I have chosen for this plant is from Luke's account of the birth of Jesus. It is the narrative of the shepherds and the angels:

> *And there were shepherds living out in the fields nearby, keeping watch over their flocks at night. An angel of the Lord appeared to them, and the glory of the Lord shone around them, and they were terrified. But the angel said to them, "Do not be afraid. I bring you good news of great joy that will be for all the people. Today in the town of David a Savior has been born to you; he is Christ the Lord."*
>
> *(Luke 2:8–11 NIV)*

This is one of my favorites! Its colors are magnificent—red just as beautiful as you would imagine. It's a 25–inch-tall repeat bloomer, a velvety good true red with burgundy veining and shading. The rib is flat and a slightly lighter red. Its small yellow-green throat is brushed one-third of the way up on the rib. By 7:30 p.m. after a sunny, warm day, the burgundy veining fades some, but the flower is a pure "tart cherry" red. This is a very pretty flower.

Bible Story

One of the Bible first stories we were taught as children was the one about Jonah and the whale. What an impact that story has had on children throughout the ages. I have chosen that story to be the "Bible Story" that relates to this plant. Let's review the wonderful verses from the book of Jonah:

> *Now the Lord had prepared a great fish to swallow up Jonah. And Jonah was in the belly of the fish three days and three nights. Then Jonah prayed unto the Lord his God out of the fish's belly. And the word of the Lord came unto Jonah the second time, saying, Arise, go unto Nineveh, that great city, and preach unto it the preaching that I bid thee.*
> *(Jonah 1:17, 2:1, 3:1–2 KJV)*

This is another one of the beautiful pink daylilies. It is 30 inches tall and has a 3–inch flower. The cream pink color is excellent.

Joel

The book of Joel was written about 8 or 9 B.C. The name "Joel" means "The Lord Jehovah." His book is split into three parts. The first is about the present chastisement and its removal, the second is the promise of the Spirit, and the third is the future deliverance in the coming days of the Lord. We are today seeing the fulfillment of the scripture that Joel was prophesying. Let's review that scripture:

And it shall come to pass afterward, that I will pour out my spirit upon all flesh; and your sons and your daughters shall prophesy, your old men shall dream dreams, your young men shall see visions: And also upon the servants and upon the handmaids in those days will I pour out my spirit.

(Joel 2:28–29 KJV)

The daylily "Joel" is a bright lemon yellow. This plant would go wonderfully with other yellow daylilies such as "Noah's Ark" or the "Harp of David."

Diary of Faith

Just where in the Bible would one find a "Diary of Faith"? As you look through the scriptures and come to the book of Hebrews, you will find an excellent example. Who wrote this diary? No one knows, as the author of the book of Hebrews is unknown.

> *Now faith is the substance of things hoped for, the evidence of things not seen. For by it the elders obtained a good report. Through faith we understand that the worlds were framed by the word of God, so that things which are seen were not made of things which do appear.*
> *(Hebrews 11:1–3 KJV)*

Really, you should read the entire wonderful chapter of Hebrews 11. It's great. The daylily that is named for this beautiful passage is 24 inches tall with a 5–inch flower. It is orchid cream in color.

Yellow Angel

Would you ever think that a yellow angel would be mentioned in the Bible? I'll help you out with this one. Remember the description of the angel who appeared to Mary Magdalene and the other Mary when they went to Jesus' tomb at dawn two days after the Crucifixion? Let's read those verses of scripture now and see the angel who might have appeared to be yellow:

> *After the Sabbath, at dawn on the first day of the week, Mary Magdalene and the other Mary went to look at the tomb. There was a violent earthquake, for an angel of the Lord came down from heaven and, going to the tomb, rolled back the stone and sat on it. His appearance was like lightning, and his clothes were white as snow.*
>
> *(Matthew 28:1–6 NIV)*

Well now, that is a yellow angel. As you would imagine, this plant has a big, beautiful yellow flower. It grows to be 30 inches tall and is a really nice plant with many blossoms.

Easter Sunday

This is very interesting. While looking throughout the Bible for a verse that would reflect the meaning of this daylily, I was using the Living Bible. Now the Living Bible tells the same message of the resurrection that we just saw in the previous daylily (Yellow Angel); however, it starts out with early Sunday morning—that is certainly Easter Sunday as we know it. Let's read the account in the gospel of John from the Living Bible:

> *Early Sunday morning, while it was still dark, Mary Magdalene came to the tomb and found that the stone was rolled aside from the entrance. She ran and found Simon Peter and me and said, "They have taken the Lord's body out of the tomb, and I don't know where they have put him!" We ran to the tomb to see; I outran Peter and got there first, and stooped and looked in and saw the linen cloth lying there, but I didn't go in. Then Simon Peter arrived and went on inside.*
>
> *(John 20:1–6 TLB)*

Now isn't that interesting? What kind of daylily is this "Easter Sunday"? Just as you might imagine, it is a gold flower—a large, beautiful gold self with a green throat and a six-inch flower. The bloom is pie-crusted and ruffled. It would go really nicely with the just mentioned "Yellow Angel."

Mission Choir

For this plant I had to find a scripture passage that tells of a choir on a mission. I found a choir of angels that was on a mission to tell the shepherds about the birth of Jesus. Let's read those wonderful Christmas verses now, and you will see the Mission Choir:

> *Suddenly, the angel was joined by a vast host of others—the armies of heaven—praising God: "Glory to God in the highest heaven," they sang, "and peace on earth for all those pleasing him." When this great army of angels had returned again to heaven, the shepherds said to each other, "Come on! Let's go to Bethlehem! Let's see this wonderful thing that has happened, which the Lord has told about."*
> *(Luke 2:13–15 TLB)*

Angel's Delight

Where in the Bible did the angels have the best delight? My first thought was to go to the scriptures on the birth of Christ. Then I went to the resurrection scriptures to seek the delight of angels. Finally, I went to the book of Revelation and found what I think are the greatest verses concerning the "Angel's Delight." Let's read the following passage:

> *Then in my vision I heard the singing of millions of angels surrounding the throne and the Living Beings and the Elders: "The Lamb is worthy" (loudly they sang it!) "—the Lamb who was slain. He is worthy to receive the power, and the riches, and the wisdom, and the strength, and the honor, and the glory, and the blessing."*
> *(Revelation 5:11–12 TLB)*

Angel's Delight is a very simple but beautiful peach-colored daylily. It has a four-inch bloom. The peach color is a real treat in the garden.

Angel Glow

In the book of Isaiah, we find the prophet's vision or commission. I sought this verse because it certainly describes the angels—and I'm sure they had a glow to them:

> *In the year that King Uzziah died, I saw the Lord seated on a throne, high and exalted, and the train of his robe filled the temple. Above him were seraphs, each with six wings: With two wings they covered their faces, with two they covered their feet, and with two they were flying. And they were calling to one another: "Holy, holy, holy is the Lord Almighty; the whole earth is full of his glory."*
> *(Isaiah 6:1–3 NIV)*

How is that for a description of "Angel Glow"? What color would you think this flower would be? It's a beautiful true pink. Put this with some white daylilies and you'll have a little bit of heaven in your garden!

Heaven's Pride

If you look in the book of Revelation, you will find the scriptures that tell of the New Jerusalem. That certainly is the new earth, or you might call it "Heaven's Pride." Let's review those verses and see if you do not agree!

Then I saw a new heaven and a new earth, for the first heaven and the first earth had passed away, and there was no longer any sea. I saw the Holy City, the new Jerusalem, coming down out of heaven from God, prepared as a bride beautifully dressed for her husband. And I heard a loud voice from the throne saying, "Now the dwelling of God is with men, and he will live with them. They will be his people, and God himself will be with them and be their God."
(Revelation 21:1–3 NIV)

Just as you would expect, this is a beautiful creation. Its color is a soft yellow with a light bronze halo. It is heavily ruffled with light bronze edges. You would be proud of "Heaven's Pride."

Praise the Lord

This phrase is used often to give praise to the Lord for all he does for us on a continuing basis. What a good God we have, knowing that he rules over us from his kingdom above. As I sought the best scripture to go with this mighty flower, I came across those wonderful verses in the Psalms that reflect "Praise the Lord":

> *The Lord has established his throne in heaven, and his kingdom rules over all. Praise the Lord, you his angels, you mighty ones who do his bidding, who obey his word. Praise the Lord, all his heavenly hosts, you his servants who do his will. Praise the Lord, all his works everywhere in his dominion. Praise the Lord, O my soul.*
>
> *(Psalm 103:19–22 NIV)*

The daylily named after this powerful phrase is a beautiful medium rose pink. It's a grand flower about 25 inches tall and will seem to say, "Praise the Lord" whenever you see it. It's a nice addition to any garden.

Glory Hallelujah

I think that the nineteenth chapter of the book of Revelation might just be called the "Hallelujah" chapter! Looking for scripture that mentions both "glory" and "hallelujah," I found both of those great words in Revelation 19. Let's read them now:

> *Then I heard what sounded like a great multitude, like the roar of rushing waters and like loud peals of thunder, shouting: "Hallelujah! For our Lord God Almighty reigns. Let us rejoice and be glad and give him glory!"*
> *(Revelation 19:6–7 NIV)*

This daylily is very attractive with its rose-brown color and a purple-red eye. It is a good size, growing to about 24 inches. It's very pretty in the garden. A special color.

Gentle Blessing

It was enjoyable to search for what would be a good example of a gentle blessing! Reading the Bible one Sunday afternoon, I found myself in the book of Ephesians. I was there because that morning at church, the visiting preacher gave his sermon from that book of the Bible. As I started to read from this letter, written by the Apostle Paul, there it was—the answer to my search for the "Gentle Blessing." Let's read it now:

Dear Christian friends at Ephesus, ever loyal to the Lord: This is Paul writing to you, chosen by God to be Jesus Christ's messenger. May his blessings and peace be yours, sent to you from God our Father and Jesus Christ our Lord. How we praise God, the Father of our Lord Jesus Christ, who has blessed us with every blessing in heaven because we belong to Christ.
(Ephesians 1:1–3 TLB)

This is one of those big, beautiful, near-white daylilies that look so wonderful in a garden. It would look even more striking if it were planted with the daylily "Praise the Lord," with that nice rose pink. It's a nice tall flower, growing to be about 33 inches. I love mine.

Glory Days

As I thought of this name, I was quickened that the "Glory Days" will surely be in heaven and will last forever! I found two verses that are so similar in words that they both need to be used. What is more interesting is that two different apostles wrote these scriptures—Paul and John. Let's look at these two verses and see if you can see the "Glory Days":

Yes, and the Lord will always deliver me from all evil and will bring me into his heavenly Kingdom. To God be the glory forever and ever. Amen.
(2 Timothy 4:18 TLB)

He has gathered us into his Kingdom and made us priests of God his Father. Give to him everlasting glory! He rules forever! Amen!
(Revelation 1:6 TLB)

Well, we know that our glory days will last forever. You will want this beautiful gold flower to last a long time also. It's gold, just like we will find when we get to glory ourselves.

Prayer Time

Prayer is mentioned a lot in the Bible; however, there is only one mention of a specific time for prayer. As you read the book of Acts, you will find that specific time. Let's read it at this time:

Peter and John went to the Temple one afternoon to take part in the three o'clock daily prayer meeting.
(Acts 3:1 TLB)

This is another beautiful peach-colored flower that adds so much to a daylily garden. It's a plant that blooms early, just about when the last iris finishes its yearly blooming season.

Royal Rapture

What will it be like? We hear about the rapture and we know it will happen, but how long will it take? For the answer to those questions and the best verse for this particular plant, I refer you to Paul's first letter to the Corinthians:

> *Listen, I tell you a mystery: We will not all sleep, but we will all be changed—in a flash, in the twinkling of an eye, at the last trumpet. For the trumpet will sound, the dead will be raised imperishable, and we will be changed. For the perishable must clothe itself with the imperishable, and the mortal with immortality.*
>
> *(1 Corinthians 15:51–53 NIV)*

This is a scintillating burgundy wine colored flower with a large chartreuse throat. Adding to its beauty are the ruffled petals with beige edging. It usually has fifteen buds and blooms that are six inches round.

Blessed Assurance

What is our blessed assurance, and who is it for? Well, if you look in the Bible, you will find one verse that tells just that. Let's read it now:

> ***Those who have served well gain an excellent standing and great assurance in their faith in Christ Jesus.***
>
> ***(1 Timothy 3:13 NIV)***

This is a very tall, 36–inch flower with a great rose-pink color. Its height and striking color give us that feeling of assurance. It deserves a place in the back of your garden with a nice white daylily (such as "Gentle Blessing") in front of it. What a great combination of both colors and words!

Almost Heaven

"Almost" is a term used to describe something missed, as in a game of horseshoes. In that game, "almost" doesn't count. The football that was "almost" caught does not count as a touchdown, and so on. It's the same way for going to heaven! "Almost Heaven" is not heaven—no points, no score, no heaven at all. Let's see the verses that talk about the rich young man who got his instruction from Jesus on how to inherit eternal life:

> *As Jesus started on his way, a man ran up to him and fell on his knees before him. "Good teacher," he asked, "what must I do to inherit eternal life?" Jesus looked at him and loved him. "One thing you lack," he said. "Go, sell everything you have and give to the poor, and you will have treasure in heaven. Then come, follow me."*
>
> *(Mark 10:17, 21 NIV)*

This is a late bloomer when it comes to daylilies. It has a nice cream-tinted pink color that is beautiful. It will grow to be about 24 inches tall and looks really nice in the garden, especially with the rose-pink flowers of "Blessed Assurance" or "Agape Love."

Apostle Matthew

The apostle Matthew was by profession a tax collector. Let's look at Mark's gospel as it describes the call of Matthew:

> *As he walked along, he saw Levi son of Alphaeus sitting at the tax collector's booth. "Follow me," Jesus told him, and Levi got up and followed him.*
> *(Mark 2:14 NIV)*

We know that Jesus later changed Levi's name to Matthew. What is so striking about this calling is how obedient Matthew was to the Lord's call, even though he was a sinner. Jesus later used this to teach the Pharisees that he did not come to call the righteous, but the sinners to repent.

This daylily is a beauty! It is a show of different colors that begins its bloom in the morning and remains until late evening. It is one of the fragrant daylilies with six-inch flowers. Just think of the beauty as the colors are described. It is a very ruffled light peach with light gold veining and light burnt sienna shading from the edges of the segments into the bloom. The shading is lightly brushed across the segments just above the wide yellow-green throat. The wide raised pink rib runs into a green heart. It is edged in melon. It will grow to be 28 inches high and will bloom in midseason.

Archangel

Did you know that "archangel" is mentioned only twice in the Bible? But, as you read this book, you will find many, many flowers and plants that have the name "Archangel." You can just see and feel the power of might and strength in these verses taken from 1 Thessalonians:

> *For the Lord himself will come down from heaven, with a loud command, with the voice of the archangel and with the trumpet call of God, and the dead in Christ will rise first. After that, we who are still alive and are left will be caught up together with them in the clouds to meet the Lord in the air. And so we will be with the Lord forever.*
> *(1 Thessalonians 4:16–17 NIV)*

This daylily is a real beauty. It won a Junior Citation in 1977 and then an Award of Merit in 1980 by the American Hemerocallis Society. "Archangel" is one of the most beautiful, if not the most beautiful, cantaloupe- or melon-colored blossom in the garden. It is light orange with lavender raised ribs going deep into a brilliant yellow heart. Blooms open wide, leaving a shallow heart; sepals curve with a twist. One of the best you can have in your garden. It will grow to be 20 to 24 inches tall with 7– to 8–inch blooms.

Acres of Angels

We do not really know how many angels there are. I believe, though, that there are many acres of them.

Praise him, all his angels, praise him, all his heavenly hosts.

(Psalm 148:2 NIV)

As we review the colors of this flower you'll see why it was given the name "Acres of Angels." This 32–inch plant blooms from morning to late evening. It is a lovely yellow pastel blended with pink. A small green heart is set at the depths of its brilliant greenish yellow throat that radiates onto segments. It has a very definite yellow edging on extremely riffled petals. Excellent.

Glory Glory

Did you know that the word "glory" is mentioned in the Bible 295 times? In one very powerful verse, it is mentioned twice. I like to think of that verse when I look at this special daylily:

If anyone is ashamed of me and my words, the Son of Man will be ashamed of him when he comes in his glory and in the glory of the Father and of the holy angels.

(Luke 9:26 NIV)

The flower named "Glory Glory" is just what you would imagine. A real beauty—very creped, ruffled, pie-crusted cream with light yellow veining and shading; a near-white rib runs through the wide yellow-green throat into a green heart. "Glory Glory" belongs in any garden, especially a church garden.

Lifted Hands

In Leviticus 9, we read about the priests beginning their ministry. Let's read that scripture now:

> *Then Aaron lifted his hands toward the people and blessed them. And having sacrificed the sin offering, the burnt offering and the fellowship offering, he stepped down.*
>
> *(Leviticus 9:22 NIV)*

This is 30 inches tall and blooms all day long with a 5-inch blossom. It is cream with a raised cream rib and yellow veining; it has a deep green heart in the morning that turns to yellow in the evening. As you look at this flower, you can imagine the hands of Aaron lifted up as he blessed the people.

Prayer Time

We all know that any time is prayer time. There is one particular Bible verse that mentions a specific time that Peter and John went to the temple to pray:

> *One day Peter and John were going up to the temple at the time of prayer—at three in the afternoon.*
> *(Acts 3:1 NIV)*

This is an excellent flower that needs water during the growing season. Perhaps that's where the prayer time had its influence on this beauty. This plant is one of the special fragrant ones. Its color is a delicate peach with darker peach edging; lavender raised ribs run into the depths of its green heart. It is excellent.

Eternal Fire

The words "eternal fire" are mentioned in the Bible three different times. Each verse talks about our lives on earth and the consequences of not living according to the Bible. Let's review these powerful verses:

If your hand or your foot causes you to sin, cut it off and throw it away. It is better for you to enter life maimed or crippled than to have two hands or two feet and be thrown into eternal fire.

(Matthew 18:8 NIV)

Then he will say to those on his left, "Depart from me, you who are cursed, into the eternal fire prepared for the devil and his angels."

(Matthew 25:41 NIV)

In a similar way, Sodom and Gomorrah and the surrounding towns gave themselves up to sexual immorality and perversion. They serve as an example of those who suffer the punishment of eternal fire.

(Jude 7 NIV)

It is interesting to read the description of the flower. It is a light yellow apricot with **fire from the heart!** It is a 30–inch flower that blooms from daybreak to the evening. It repeats its blooms of five- to six-inch size. The flowers are round crimped, ruffled, and heavily creped. It's good to have in your church garden for those Sunday morning Bible studies. What a lesson.

Heavenly Harp

Harps are mentioned many times in the Bible. I think the verse that best describes a "heavenly harp" is one taken from the book of Psalms. Let's read it now:

> ***Then will I go to the altar of God, to God, my joy and my delight. I will praise you with the harp, O God, my God.***
>
> ***(Psalm 43:4 NIV)***

This is a beautiful flower that won Honorable Mention in 1969 by the American Hemerocallis Society. It certainly is a description of heaven. It is 28 to 32 inches tall and repeats its bloom. It blooms from early morning to late evening and is fragrant. The colors are creamy yellow overlaid with gold. It has bright pink ribs and a flush of intense rose pink at the petal tips. It has a ruffled gold edge and glossy finish, adding to its beauty.

Sabbath Eve

In the Bible, in the book of Exodus chapter 16, the Lord tells Moses that he will rain down bread from heaven for him. Moses then told the people in the desert about this "manna," as he talked about the "Sabbath eve":

> *He said to them, "This is what the Lord commanded: 'Tomorrow is to be a day of rest, a holy Sabbath to the Lord. So bake what you want to bake and boil what you want to boil. Save whatever is left and keep it until morning.'"*
>
> *(Exodus 16:23 NIV)*

Wiseman

Wise men are not mentioned in the Bible; however, since we were all little children, we have been told about the wise men who visited the baby Jesus and brought gifts. The Bible refers to these visitors as Magi. Let's read from Matthew about the visit of the Magi:

> *After Jesus was born in Bethlehem in Judea, during the time of King Herod, Magi from the east came to Jerusalem and asked, "Where is the one who has been born king of the Jews? We saw his star in the east and have come to worship him."*
> *(Matthew 2:1–2 NIV)*

This is another beautiful fragrant daylily that is a repeat bloomer. It has a five-inch bloom, is ruffled, velvety magenta with burgundy veining and shading, has a lavender raised rib, and has a small green gold throat. In the morning the color is very rich and velvety. The rounded petals overlap and are slightly pinched and raised at the ends; the sepals are greatly curved. This is another one of the plants that could be used for the Sunday morning Bible school for children—of all ages!

Gift of Grace

No other verse in the Bible more accurately describes the real gift of grace better than the one in Romans where death through Adam and life through Christ are proclaimed. Let's read that wonderful verse now:

> *But the gift is not like the trespass. For if the many died by the trespass of the one man, how much more did God's grace and the gift that came by the grace of the one man, Jesus Christ, overflow to the many!*
>
> *(Romans 5:15 NIV)*

Just listen to the description of this beauty. It is a diamond-dusted and ruffled cream color with a peach blush. Its raised rib runs to a green heart. It has a large, closed star shape and is a fragrant bloomer. It is a 23–inch tall plant with a large 6+–inch bloom.

Blessed Joy

The words "blessed" and "joy" are mentioned in the Bible many times, but never together. As you read the Bible, you cannot help but see those words reflecting the great rapture. Let's read the two verses that to me best put these two wonderful words together:

> *Blessed and holy are those who share in the First Resurrection. For them the Second Death holds no terrors, for they will be priests of God and of Christ, and shall reign with him a thousand years.*
>
> *(Revelation 20:6 TLB)*

> *You love him even though you have never seen him; though not seeing him, you trust him; and even now you are happy with the inexpressible joy that comes from heaven itself.*
>
> *(1 Peter 1:8 TLB)*

This is an excellent 26–inch daylong bloomer that has a 6–inch flower and is fragrant. It is very ruffled, creped light yellow with pale peach veining and pale peach raised rib that runs through a yellow-green throat. There is a peach blush on either side of the rib one-third of the way up the petals. This is a beauty.

Commandment

I think the best verse reflecting "commandment" is the one in Joshua where he called together the tribes of Reuben, Gad, and the half-tribe of Manasseh, and addressed them, reminding them to keep and obey the commandments. Let's read the verse from Joshua:

> *Be sure to continue to obey all of the commandments Moses gave you. Love the Lord and follow his plan for your lives. Cling to him and serve him enthusiastically.*
>
> *(Joshua 22:5 TLB)*

This flower is a tetraploid, which means it has 44 chromosomes to the cell instead of 22. It is a repeat bloomer that won the Award of Merit (won by only 10 daylilies each year) in 1977, and in 1972 it won Honorable Mention as an introduced variety. This is an excellent flower with rich, deep buff-apricot to tangerine-orange and an exceptionally smooth finish; its great rounded segments are very broad. This is a must for your church or home garden!

୧୨

Agape Love

What is love? It certainly is not what we were led to believe from the movie *Love Story* from the 1970s. The Bible is full of love stories—stories of God's love for us. He loved us so much—remember John 3:16? Let's look at another Bible verse about love:

> *This is love: not that we loved God, but that he loved us and sent his Son as an atoning sacrifice for our sins. Dear friends, since God so loved us, we also ought to love one another. No one has ever seen God; but if we love one another, God lives in us and his love is made complete in us.*
>
> *(1 John 4:10–12 NIV)*

The colors of this plant say "love." It is ivory with pink ribs, and with its rather short height, it looks just like a bouquet of flowers. It's great in the front of your garden, and it says, "I love you" to all who look at it.

Isaac

Isaac is mentioned in the Bible many times. It is interesting to note that the first time he is mentioned, God established a covenant with him and for his descendants after him:

> ***Then God said, "Yes, but your wife Sarah will bear you a son, and you will call him Isaac. I will establish my covenant with him as an everlasting covenant for his descendants after him."***
>
> ***(Genesis 17:19 NIV)***

This is another beautiful award winner (Honorable Mention—1976). It blooms from early morning until late evening with beautiful yellow flowers that resemble an umbrella. The 4–inch blooms on this 26– to 28–inch tall plant would enhance any garden.

Worthy One

This is absolutely shouted out to us in the Bible! Let's get right into that verse:

> *For great is the Lord and most worthy of praise;*
> *he is to be feared above all gods.*
> *(1 Chronicles 16:25 NIV)*

This is absolutely one of the best daylilies you can have. Why not, with a name like "Worthy One"? It features a double, fragrant five-inch flower that blooms all day, and in fact will change colors as the day goes on. It is ruffled, creped burgundy (dark burgundy in the morning) with a self-colored flat rib with a tiny cream line in the center of the rib and the sepals. It is usually loaded with buds.

Emanual (Immanuel)

Here is a daylily called "Emanual." We know that the spelling in the Bible is "Immanuel" and is found in Matthew's account of the birth of Jesus. Remember the Christmas song, "O Come, O Come Emmanuel"? Let's read that verse from the apostle Matthew:

> *"The virgin will be with child and will give birth to a son, and they will call him Immanuel"—which means, "God with us."*
>
> *(Matthew 1:23 NIV)*

This flower is a colorful one, just like you might find hanging from a Christmas tree. Listen to the bright color description: extremely velvety, ruffled, slightly creped cherry red with burgundy rib, veining, and shading. It has a small triangular yellow throat and a green heart. It has a 6–inch bloom and will grow to be 28 to 32 inches tall. Excellent.

Spiritual Bouquet

In Isaiah, there is a reading on the "joy of the redeemed" where the beauty of the flowers is told. Certainly we will all see many, many bouquets of flowers in heaven. Let's read from the book of Isaiah about the flowers we will be seeing:

Even the wilderness and desert will rejoice in those days; the desert will blossom with flowers. Yes, there will be an abundance of flowers and singing and joy! The deserts will become as green as the Lebanon mountains, as lovely as Mount Carmel's pastures and Sharon's meadows; for the Lord will display his glory there, the excellency of our God.
(Isaiah 35:1–2 TLB)

This is a lavender-colored bloom. It is an early bloomer and is only 13 inches tall. When in bloom, it probably looks like a "bouquet." It's a nice flower.

Gentle Shepherd

This is an easy one. Everybody knows the 23rd Psalm and how it talks about how the Lord is our shepherd. Let's read that wonderful scripture now in its entirety:

> *The Lord is my shepherd, I shall not be in want.*
> *He makes me lie down in green pastures, he leads me beside quiet waters, he restores my soul.*
> *He guides me in paths of righteousness for his name's sake.*
> *Even though I walk through the valley of the shadow of death,*
> *I will fear no evil, for you are with me; your rod and your staff, they comfort me.*
> *You prepare a table before me in the presence of my enemies.*
> *You anoint my head with oil; my cup overflows.*
> *Surely goodness and love will follow me all the days of my life, and I will dwell in the house of the Lord forever.*
>
> *(Psalm 23 NIV)*

Well now, just what color do you think this "Gentle Shepherd" would be? Yes, it's white just like the lamb that the shepherd watches over. It's a beautiful flower that won an award in 1981 for excellence. It has a 5–inch bloom on a 29–inch-tall stem. It's great in a garden and mixes with any other color.

Glorious Grace

We do have "glorious grace" that was given to us as a spiritual blessing. The apostle Paul writes about that gift in Ephesians. Let's read that verse that puts these two wonderful words together:

> *In love he predestined us to be adopted as his sons through Jesus Christ, in accordance with his pleasure and will—to the praise of his glorious grace, which he has freely given us in the One he loves.*
> *(Ephesians 1:4–6 NIV)*

This is a star-shaped flower, just as glorious as grace would look. Listen to this "glorious" description: a 24–inch plant with a 7–inch bloom. It's a ruffled and lightly creped rose color with fuchsia veining and shading in its ruffles and a raised rose rib. Its large wide triangular yellow throat ends in very faint light burgundy watermarks. It is a large, semiairy star shape. This is an excellent beauty for your church or personal garden.

Eternal

How long is eternal? Well, it's forever, isn't it? As I was looking through the Bible for the proper verse for this flower, I ran across the scripture where Moses blessed the tribes, which is in Deuteronomy. Let's read it now:

> ***The eternal God is your refuge, and underneath are the everlasting arms. He will drive out your enemy before you, saying, "Destroy him!"***
> ***(Deuteronomy 33:27 NIV)***

This is what is called an "excellent" flower. Its cherry-red color with burgundy ribs is about as beautiful a daylily as you can have. The bloom measures 6 inches and sits on a 32–inch-tall stem. It is especially great with a white flower to go with it. Try it with "Gentle Shepherd."

Noah's Ark

This is another one of those plants that can be used for a summer Sunday Bible school program for children (of all ages). Let's read the Genesis account of God's instruction to Noah on building the ark:

> *So God said to Noah, "I am going to put an end to all people, for the earth is filled with violence because of them. I am surely going to destroy both them and the earth. So make yourself an ark of cypress wood; make rooms in it and coat it with pitch inside and out. This is how you are to build it: The ark is to be 450 feet long, 75 feet wide and 45 feet high."*
> *(Genesis 6:13–15 NIV)*

This plant is a creamy peach pink overlaid with gold. It's a huge fragrant 7–inch flower that will grow to be 34 inches tall. It's a tetraploid that blooms at midseason. Put it outside the children's church for their enjoyment.

Barnabas

As you read the book of Acts in the Bible, you will find a narration of Barnabas's travels as he was sent by the Holy Spirit along with Saul (Paul) to teach about the Lord. His travels sent him to Cyprus, Paphos, Perga, Iconium, and then to Lystra, Derbe, and other cities in the Holy Land. Let's read the first part of Acts 13 that tells of Barnabas and Paul being sent off:

> *In the church at Antioch there were prophets and teachers: Barnabas, Simeon called Niger, Lucius of Cyrene, Manaen (who had been brought up with Herod the tetrarch) and Saul. While they were worshiping the Lord and fasting, the Holy Spirit said, "Set apart for me Barnabas and Saul for the work to which I have called them." So after they had fasted and prayed, they placed their hands on them and sent them off.*
>
> *(Acts 13:1–3 NIV)*

This plant is a wonderful yellow beauty. It has a large blossom and will grow to be about 30 inches tall. It's a great addition to any garden.

Golden Angel

There are many daylilies named after angels, but I never find it difficult to locate a verse that relates to a particular flower. Let's see the verse that talks about a "golden angel":

> *I turned around to see the voice that was speaking to me. And when I turned I saw seven golden lampstands, and among the lampstands was someone "like a son of man," dressed in a robe reaching down to his feet and with a golden sash around his chest. "Write, therefore, what you have seen, what is now and what will take place later. The mystery of the seven stars that you saw in my right hand and of the seven golden lampstands is this: The seven stars are the angels of the seven churches, and the seven lampstands are the seven churches."*
> *(Revelation 1:12–13, 19–20 NIV)*

Just like an angel, this is a diamond-dusted beauty. It's a 26–inch-tall repeat bloomer with a great fragrance. The six-inch bloom is golden yellow with deep ruffled petals. It has top multiple branching. It looks like an angel!

℃℥

Malachi

"Malachi" means "my messenger." This is the last book of the Old Testament and contains the prophecy of John the Baptist's ministry. Malachi was written about the fifth century B.C. Apart from the meaning of his name, nothing is known about him.

An oracle: The word of the Lord to Israel through Malachi.

(Malachi 1:1 NIV)

This plant is tetraploid. It has a nice burgundy color and looks just great when mixed in with the beautiful "Glory Glory" white or the "Gift of Grace" diamond-dusted cream color. This is a must for your church or home garden.

Jerusalem

When I think of Jerusalem, I always think of the New Jerusalem. Let's look at the passage in the book of Revelation that talks about that wonderful new city:

> *One of the seven angels who had the seven bowls full of the seven last plagues came and said to me, "Come, I will show you the bride, the wife of the Lamb." And he carried me away in the Spirit to a mountain great and high, and showed me the Holy City, Jerusalem, coming down out of heaven from God. It shone with the glory of God, and its brilliance was like that of a very precious jewel, like a jasper, clear as crystal.*
>
> *(Revelation 21:9–11 NIV)*

This plant is a tetraploid. It is bright gold (what else would it be?) with a yellow-green throat. It grows to be 28 inches tall with a bloom of 5 inches with extended blooming.

Amen Corner

This is best found in Deuteronomy where the verses describe the curses from Mount Ebal. If there ever was an "amen corner," surely it is as follows:

The Levites shall recite to all the people of Israel in a loud voice:

"Cursed is the man who carves an image or casts an idol—a thing detestable to the Lord, the work of the craftsman's hands—and sets it up in secret." Then all the people shall say, "Amen!"

"Cursed is the man who dishonors his father or his mother." Then all the people shall say, "Amen!"

"Cursed is the man who moves his neighbor's boundary stone." Then all the people shall say, "Amen!"

"Cursed is the man who leads the blind astray on the road." Then all the people shall say, "Amen!"

"Cursed is the man who withholds justice from the alien, the fatherless or the widow." Then all the people shall say, "Amen!"

"Cursed is the man who sleeps with his father's wife, for he dishonors his father's bed." Then all the people shall say, "Amen!"

"Cursed is the man who has sexual relations with any animal." Then all the people shall say, "Amen!"

"Cursed is the man who sleeps with his sister, the daughter of his father or the daughter of his mother." Then all the people shall say, "Amen!"

"Cursed is the man who sleeps with his mother-in-law." Then all the people shall say, "Amen!"

"Cursed is the man who kills his neighbor secretly." Then all the people shall say, "Amen!"

"Cursed is the man who accepts a bribe to kill an innocent person." Then all the people shall say, "Amen!"

"Cursed is the man who does not uphold the words of this law by carrying them out." Then all the people shall say, "Amen!"

(Deuteronomy 27:14–26 NIV)

This is one of those beautiful flame-red daylilies that add so much color to your garden. Mix it with some of the white or pink flowers and it's a real treat.

Rahab

This is an interesting Bible study. Rahab has a very important role in the Bible. One of the parts of scripture that talks about her and the spies is especially worth reading. Let's look at that story from Joshua:

> *Rahab went up to talk to the men before they retired for the night.*
>
> *"I know perfectly well that your God is going to give my country to you," she told them. "We are all afraid of you; everyone is terrified if the word Israel is even mentioned. For we have heard how the Lord made a path through the Red Sea for you when you left Egypt! And we know what you did to Sihon and Og, the two Amorite kings east of the Jordan, and how you ruined their land and completely destroyed their people. No wonder we are afraid of you! No one has any fight left in him after hearing things like that, for your God is the supreme God of heaven, not just an ordinary god.*
>
> *(Joshua 2:8–11 TLB)*

This is a very special flower. It has many very rare characteristics such as it is very fragrant, has extra blooming abilities, and is a repeat bloomer. Wow! It is flamingo a pink color with a 5–inch blossom and grows to be 25 inches tall. Its fragrance and color make it a must for any garden.

Guardian Angel

The guardian angel in the Bible that is found in Ezekiel is, in fact, a fallen angel. Just review the following scripture and see the change that came over the guardian cherub and what happened to him:

> *You were anointed as a guardian cherub, for so I ordained you. You were on the holy mount of God; you walked among the fiery stones. You were blameless in your ways from the day you were created till wickedness was found in you. Through your widespread trade you were filled with violence, and you sinned. So I drove you in disgrace from the mount of God, and I expelled you, O guardian cherub, from among the fiery stones.*
> *(Ezekiel 28:14–16 NIV)*

This plant is rather small, only three inches in size and is moderately ruffled. Its color is creamy flesh. The throat is olive colored at the base. It will grow to be about 20 inches tall.

Smiling Angel

Did you know that angels are mentioned over two hundred times in the Bible? Which one was a smiling angel? We could look up all the verses that speak of angels; however, I think you would agree with me as we read about the angel that Luke tells about in his Christmas writing that this angel had to be smiling:

> *But the angel reassured them. "Don't be afraid!"*
> *he said. "I bring you the most joyful news ever*
> *announced, and it is for everyone! The Savior—yes,*
> *the Messiah, the Lord—has been born tonight in*
> *Bethlehem!"*
> *(Luke 2:10–11 TLB)*

Now, that was a smiling angel. Wow, just listen to the description of this flower—it's just like an angel would look. It is fringed, slightly ruffled, creped light rose with peach veining and delicate lavender shading along the edges of the segments. The segment centers are light pink. It has a wide yellow-green throat and green heart. In the evening the blooms are a darker pink color. It is loaded with buds and beauty. The name surely matches the flower. It is 20 inches tall and is fragrant, which is an even better angel attraction.

Christmas Showcase

As I was looking for just the right "angel" for the previous daylily, I recognized the verses in Luke that tell of a real showcase. I'm talking about the beautiful event when the host of the armies of heaven all came down to sing praises to God. That, to me, is a real Christmas showcase. Let's read those wonderful verses:

> *Suddenly, the angel was joined by a vast host of others—the armies of heaven—praising God: "Glory to God in the highest heaven," they sang, "and peace on earth for all those pleasing him." When this great army of angels had returned again to heaven, the shepherds said to each other, "Come on! Let's go to Bethlehem! Let's see this wonderful thing that has happened, which the Lord has told us about."*
> *(Luke 2:13–15 TLB)*

This is a real Christmas flower with its very velvety, very brilliant, bright red bloom. It even has a ribbon of yellow around a lime green heart. Its ruffled, crimped segments make it look even more Christmas-like. It's a 30– to 32–inch-tall plant with good branching. This one even likes to be planted in partial shade! I'm sure you have a special place for this one in your garden.

God's Handicraft

Did you ever make anything? Sure you did. With your hobby, your workshop, or your occupation, you have made some kind of handicraft. Well, so did God. He made something very, very great: the earth! And just like the flower, it is big and beautiful. You do not have to look too far in the Bible to get an idea of God's handicraft. Let's read the first two verses:

> **When God began creating the heavens and the earth, the earth was a shapeless, chaotic mass, with the Spirit of God brooding over the dark vapors.**
> **(Genesis 1:1–2 TLB)**

Now let's see what kind of daylily is named after this handicraft. It's very big and beautiful! It is very ruffled light yellow with light gold veining and shading. A raised pink rib runs through the wide yellow throat into a green heart. In the afternoon, the yellow gives way to gold. Now that's a really good flower to be named after God's handicraft.

Praise Song

Did you know that praise is mentioned 340 times in the Bible? It was interesting to read the various verses that speak of praising the Lord. I think the one that best would match this flower is found in Psalm 66:

Sing to the Lord, all the earth! Sing of his glorious name! Tell the world how wonderful he is. How awe-inspiring are your deeds, O God! How great your power! No wonder your enemies surrender! All the earth shall worship you and sing of your glories.
(Psalm 66:1–4 TLB)

This is a lightly colored fragrant flower with a large seven-inch bloom. It will grow to be 28 inches tall. It's very ruffled light peach with pink shading. It has good branching and good substance.

Tender Shepherd

There is a wonderful verse in the Bible that really speaks of a "tender shepherd." It is found in Isaiah and could not be more fitting for this flower. Let's read it now:

> **He will feed his flock like a shepherd; he will carry the lambs in his arms and gently lead the ewes with young.**
>
> **(Isaiah 40:11 TLB)**

This is an award-winning tetraploid. It won an Honorable Mention (given to new introductions receiving ten or more votes) by the American Hemerocallis Society in 1987. It is a 24–inch flower with a 4–inch bloom that is lightly ruffled, with melon-colored petals and a pale orange rib. The blooms become pink under the sun. It is a gentle-looking plant just like the tender shepherd.

Harp of David

You know the problems that Saul and David had. Saul tried to kill David and was very jealous of him. David would only have to play his harp to make Saul feel better and to make the evil spirit go away. Let's read it from 1 Samuel:

> **And whenever the tormenting spirit from God troubled Saul, David would play the harp and Saul would feel better, and the evil spirit would go away.**
> **(1 Samuel 16:23 TLB)**

The "Harp of David" flower is a beautiful ivory color. It looks just great when mixed in with some of the red Christmas daylilies such as "Christmas Charm" and "Christmas Showcase."

Hosanna

First we have to find out what "hosanna" means. A search of the word reveals that it is a Hebrew expression meaning "save," which became an exclamation of praise. The chosen scripture passage for this flower comes from the book of John in the 12th chapter as he writes about Jesus' triumphal entry into Jerusalem. Let's read it now:

> *They took palm branches and went out to meet him, shouting, "Hosanna!" "Blessed is he who comes in the name of the Lord!" "Blessed is the King of Israel!" Jesus found a young donkey and sat upon it, as it is written, "Do not be afraid, O Daughter of Zion; see, your king is coming, seated on a donkey's colt."*
>
> *(John 12:13–15 NIV)*

The plant is a large beautiful mixture of golden-orange and melon. It has a large wide ruffled flower that is spectacular in the garden.

Pray for Peace

At the time of writing this book, our country was in no major war. From time to time, though, we have had many occasions to pray for peace. Sometimes the peace is just for ourselves or our families. As I looked through the Bible looking for the verse to best reflect this flower, I came across a wonderful verse in Proverbs:

> *There is deceit in the hearts of those who plot evil, but joy for those who promote peace.*
> *(Proverbs 12:20 NIV)*

This is a nice, large flower with a 6–inch bloom, a 30–inch stem, and a nearly white self with a green throat. It's special—it says "peace" all over it.

Bread of Life

We all know that Jesus is the "bread of life." It is clearly written in the Bible in the book of John. No long search for just the right verse here—it jumps right out at you! Let's read it:

> *I tell you the truth, he who believes has everlasting life. I am the bread of life. Your forefathers ate the manna in the desert, yet they died. But here is the bread that comes down from heaven, which a man may eat and not die. I am the living bread that came down from heaven. If anyone eats of this bread, he will live forever. This bread is my flesh, which I will give for the life of the world."*
> *(John 6:47–51 NIV)*

What a wonderful scripture, and what a wonderful flower to go with it. It is a 4–inch blossom of light yellow on a 26–inch stem. A nice, bright flower to have.

Chosen One

Who is your "chosen one"? It is Jesus, and it is stated just that way in the Bible. As you read the book of Isaiah, you will read the verse from chapter 42 that talks about the servant of the Lord:

> *Here is my servant, whom I uphold, my chosen*
> *one in whom I delight; I will put my Spirit on him*
> *and he will bring justice to the nations.*
> *(Isaiah 42:1 NIV)*

This is another near-white flower that has a big six-inch blossom. Try planting a bunch of different white daylilies together in a mound with a selection of white tulips and white peonies, and you will have a gorgeous white flower garden from early spring to the middle of summer.

King of Kings

You know who the King of Kings is? A great description of the rider on the white horse is given in the book of Revelation. Hallelujah!

> *I saw heaven standing open and there before me was a white horse, whose rider is called Faithful and True. With justice he judges and makes war. On his robe and on his thigh he has this name written: King of Kings and Lord of Lords.*
> *(Revelation 19:11, 16 NIV)*

This is a delightful plant that is rather short, 15 inches, but has big blossoms of 6 inches. The colors are lemon yellow and red, and when the plant is in bloom it looks like a bouquet. It is a great front border plant.

Heavenly Harmony

What do you think heaven will be like? Do you think it will be like going to a great big wonderful church? If you look in the Bible, there are verses that tell exactly what you will experience. It is found in the book of Hebrews. Let's read it:

> *But you have come to Mount Zion, to the heavenly Jerusalem, the city of the living God. You have come to thousands upon thousands of angels in joyful assembly, to the church of the firstborn, whose names are written in heaven. You have come to God, the judge of all men, to the spirits of righteous men made perfect, to Jesus the mediator of a new covenant, and to the sprinkled blood that speaks a better word than the blood of Abel.*
> *(Hebrews 12:22–24 NIV)*

Well, that is the church I'm going to attend—in heaven! This is one of the most beautiful of all the pink daylilies. It is 30 inches tall with a great 5–inch blossom. It's one of the best.

Lamb of God

We know that Jesus is the Lamb of God. The book of John makes that very clear in the first chapter. Let's read about the apostle John's experiences concerning the Lamb of God:

> *The next day John saw Jesus coming toward him and said, "Look, the Lamb of God, who takes away the sin of the world! The next day John was there again with two of his disciples. When he saw Jesus passing by, he said, "Look, the Lamb of God!"*
> *(John 1:29, 35–36 NIV)*

This is one of the first daylilies to bloom in your garden. It's an early plant with a beautiful cream pink self. It grows to be about 30 inches tall with a nice 6–inch blossom. This is really nice.

Guardian Angel

We used to hear in Sunday school and from our parents and again from Sister Mary in the sixth grade all about the guardian angels that we all had assigned to us. Well, they were right—there are angels looking out for us, and if we look in the Psalms we will find those verses. Here they are:

> *For he will command his angels concerning you to guard you in all your ways; they will lift you up in their hands, so that you will not strike your foot against a stone.*
>
> *(Psalm 91:11–12 NIV)*

This is another nearly white daylily, as it should be. Didn't you know that your guardian angel was dressed in white? This bloom measures about 4 inches on a 26-inch plant.

Sinai

This area is mentioned several times as the place where the Lord chiseled the Ten Commandments on the two stone tablets. Moses obeyed the Lord and presented himself in the morning on the mountaintop. And then when he came down from Mount Sinai, he was radiant.

When Moses came down from Mount Sinai with the two tablets of the Testimony in his hands, he was not aware that his face was radiant because he had spoken with the Lord.

(Exodus 34:29 NIV)

This is a radiant flower. Its primary color is yellow and it is dusted with a cinnamon color. It's a real treat to have in your garden. A big 6–inch bloom on top of a 26–inch growth is really nice.

Angel Band

What I wanted to find here was a band or large group of angels. We all know there are angels and many of them, but does the Bible describe of a large group of them somewhere? Wow, does it ever—just look in Daniel's seventh chapter that describes millions of them:

Millions of angels ministered to him, and hundreds of millions of people stood before him, waiting to be judged. Then the court began its session, and the books were opened.

(Daniel 7:10 TLB)

This is one of my favorites with its bright colors. It's a wonderful tangerine color with a red band—what a treat. It looks like an angel in the garden. It's only 22 inches tall with a 3–inch blossom, but is very striking.

True Glory

I relate true glory to the King of glory. As you look through the Bible to find verses describing "glory," you cannot help but be drawn to those wonderful words from the book of Psalms that talk about the "King of glory":

> *Lift up your heads, O you gates; be lifted up, you ancient doors,*
> *that the King of glory may come in. Who is this King of glory?*
> *The Lord strong and mighty, the Lord mighty in battle.*
> *Lift up your heads, O you gates; lift them up, you ancient doors,*
> *that the King of glory may come in. Who is he, this King of glory?*
> *The Lord Almighty—he is the King of glory.*
> *(Psalm 24:7–10 NIV)*

This flower is just how you would think "glory" is going to be! The color is a gold blend, very striking, with a green throat. It is 26 inches tall with a big 6–inch blossom. It's a "true glory" to have in your garden.

Angel Robes

What do you think angels are dressed in? I always wondered, and in fact thought that they were dressed in white robes. Well, that is the joy of looking through the Bible looking for the answer. I found that answer in the book of Revelation in the writings about the angel and the little scroll. Let's read it:

> *Then I saw another mighty angel coming down from heaven. He was robed in a cloud, with a rainbow above his head; his face was like the sun, and his legs were like fiery pillars.*
>
> *(Revelation 10:1 NIV)*

Well, there are no rainbow-colored daylilies, at this time anyway. This is a tall (30–inch) flower with a 5–inch blossom. Its color is a pale yellow. It's nice because it is tall and will hold its own among other daylilies in your garden.

❧

Heaven Sent

I thought that the scriptures in John that teach about Jesus calling Philip and Nathaniel was a good selection for this title. We know that Jesus himself was "heaven sent," and when he called the disciples, he just continued that process. Let's look at the reading from John:

> *Jesus said, "You believe because I told you I saw you under the fig tree. You shall see greater things than that." He then added, "I tell you the truth, you shall see heaven open, and the angels of God ascending and descending on the Son of Man."*
> *(John 1:50–51 NIV)*

This is a rare oxblood-red blend, one of the few with that coloring I have seen. It's a tall, 32–inch flower with a big 6–inch blossom. A real blend. It's a nice color, and looks beautiful with some of the white daylilies that we have talked about.

Master Plan

I love this one! This to me is the golden rule of God. We know that God has a plan for our lives, a plan that is right, true, and fair. We ought to know that we, if responsible for others, ought to have a plan to treat them as we want to be treated. Let's look at the master plan of God:

> **Masters, provide your slaves with what is right and fair, because you know that you also have a Master in heaven.**
>
> **(Colossians 4:1 NIV)**

This is a pretty flower, no doubt about it. It is a pale cream with a faint pink underlay. I like blossoms that are interesting, especially those with mixtures of colors. It's not too big—only 20 inches tall—but has a rather large flower of 6 inches.

Heavenly Guide

I always thought that as adults we do not need guides, at least in living our lives. There is a guide though—I always felt it was for children—that I have used for this particular plant name. I think you will like it! Matthew writes about the parable of the lost sheep:

> *See that you do not look down on one of these little ones. For I tell you that their angels in heaven always see the face of my Father in heaven.*
> *(Matthew 18:10 NIV)*

This daylily is another beauty. It is a delicate creamy ruffled yellow blushed pink. Not only does the name and verse remind me of a child, but the colors are just what a little child—my grandchild—would wear to church on Sunday. I love those mixtures! It's 28 inches tall with a 5–inch blossom.

Speak of Angels

What does God say about angels? Did you know that he describes his angels in the book of Hebrews? Let's read that scripture right now:

> *And again, when God brings his firstborn into the world, he says, "Let all God's angels worship him." In speaking of the angels he says, "He makes his angels winds, his servants flames of fire."*
> *(Hebrews 1:6–7 NIV)*

This is a wonderful daylily. Its colors are spectacular, being flesh pink with a soft pink lavender halo. It has a big six-inch blossom and will remind you of an angel!

Heavenly Treasure

We know that there is certainly heavenly treasure! The Bible tells of it in one of the parables in the book of Matthew. It's a great verse. Let's read it now:

> **The kingdom of heaven is like treasure hidden in a field. When a man found it, he hid it again, and then in his joy went and sold all he had and bought that field.**
>
> **(Matthew 13:44 NIV)**

Pretty—that is the word to use for this flower. It's a tall plant with a big blossom in a beautiful "very" ruffled apricot-melon blend. If you have only one Bible verse to know and one daylily to have, this is the perfect match!

Inspired Word

I think that the entire Bible is an inspired word. Trying to find a few verses that can say that was not easy. After a somewhat lengthy search, I decided to use the scripture from Ephesians that reflects how we should praise God and how we should give thanks:

> **Speak to one another with psalms, hymns and spiritual songs. Sing and make music in your heart to the Lord, always giving thanks to God the Father for everything, in the name of our Lord Jesus Christ.**
> **(Ephesians 5:19–20 NIV)**

This flower is a blend of cream yellow and lavender. It's a mid-season bloomer that looks great with a bunch of other blends and multicolored daylilies! It's inspiring to have in your garden.

King's Cloak

What kinds of clothes to you have? If you were to put to death today, do you think others would gamble to perhaps get them for their own? It is written that at the crucifixion, the soldiers did just that. I think they knew or felt that Jesus was a special person. There is no reference to the soldiers doing the same for the two robbers who were also put to death.

After the crucifixion, the soldiers threw dice to divide up his clothes among themselves. Then they sat around and watched him as he hung there. And they put a sign above his head, "This is Jesus, the King of the Jews."

(Matthew 27:35–37 TLB)

This is a beautiful magenta rose-colored daylily. It's one of the most beautiful of the repeat bloomers—twice the enjoyment. It's only 15 inches tall but has a nice 6–inch flower. Put this with a white daylily—wow!

Moment of Truth

We might all find a different scripture in the Bible that we would select to go with this name. I think that the "moment of truth" came just after the death of Jesus. Listen to what happened immediately following his earthly death:

> *Then Jesus shouted out again, dismissed his spirit, and died. And look! The curtain secluding the Holiest Place in the Temple was split apart from top to bottom; and the earth shook, and rocks broke, and tombs opened, and many godly men and women who had died came back to life again.*
> *(Matthew 27:50–52 TLB)*

This is a near-white daylily that grows to be 24 inches tall and has a 6–inch blossom. It's another repeat bloomer and is a nice flower. How about putting this with "King's Cloak," another repeat bloomer, for a great combination.

Christmas Is

This is very plainly written in the Bible. I like the scriptures that the apostle Luke uses to describe the first Christmas:

> *So Joseph also went up from the town of Nazareth in Galilee to Judea, to Bethlehem the town of David, because he belonged to the house and line of David. He went there to register with Mary, who was pledged to be married to him and was expecting a child. While they were there, the time came for the baby to be born, and she gave birth to her firstborn, a son.*
>
> *(Luke 2:4–7 NIV)*

This flower is just what you think it should be. It is a deep Christmas-red 4–inch blossom and is a repeater. It's 26 inches tall and belongs in every daylily garden!

Christening Gown

I remember our three boys and the beautiful "gowns" that they all wore for their christenings. If you're a parent, I'm sure you remember your child's gown also. It may have even been handed down from generation to generation for such occasions. I'm reading about the clothes that Jesus had at the time of his birth. Let's read from two different Bibles that describe his newborn outfit:

And she gave birth to her first child, a son. She wrapped him in a blanket and laid him in a manger, because there was no room for them in the village inn.
(Luke 2:7 TLB)

And she gave birth to her firstborn, a son. She wrapped him in cloths and placed him in a manger, because there was no room for them in the inn.
(Luke 2:7 NIV)

I also remember the wonderful "baby smell" of those newborn outfits of our children. It's only fitting that this particular daylily is a fragrant one. Also fitting is the fact that it is a creamy yellow one, appropriate for little baby boys as well as baby girls. It's a nice flower with a 6–inch blossom on top of a 26–inch stem.

Master Touch

I think the best scripture to describe the Master's touch comes from the book of Luke about the woman who wanted to be healed. She believed that if she could only touch the hem of his garment she would be healed:

> *As they went a woman who wanted to be healed came up behind and touched him, for she had been slowly bleeding for twelve years, and could find no cure (though she had spent everything she had on doctors). But the instant she touched the edge of his robe, the bleeding stopped. "Who touched me?" Jesus asked. Everyone denied it, and Peter said, "Master, so many are crowding against you. . . ." But Jesus told him, "No, it was someone who deliberately touched me, for I felt healing power go out from me."*
>
> *(Luke 8:43–46 TLB)*

This is very colorful. It is a big 6_–inch blossom with a pink self and a tangerine throat. Its stem grows to be 30 inches tall and looks great, especially with a mix of other colored daylilies.

Nebuchadnezzar's Furnace

This was, and still is, my favorite Bible story. It teaches the greatness of God's help toward us. All we need is faith. Let's read from Daniel all about that hot furnace:

> *Then Nebuchadnezzar was furious with Shadrach, Meshach and Abednego, and his attitude toward them changed. He ordered the furnace heated seven times hotter than usual and commanded some of the strongest soldiers in his army to tie up Shadrach, Meshach and Abednego and throw them into the blazing furnace. So these men, wearing their robes, trousers, turbans and other clothes, were bound and thrown into the blazing furnace. The king's command was so urgent and the furnace so hot that the flames of the fire killed the soldiers who took up Shadrach, Meshach and Abednego, and these three men, firmly tied, fell into the blazing furnace.*
>
> *(Daniel 3:19–23 NIV)*

This is one of the most beautiful of all daylilies! Listen to the colors—it's like the flower is on fire. It's a red blossom with a red eyezone. Not only that, but it is a double blossom. It has nice 5–inch blooms on top of a 22–inch stem.

Elijah

We could all learn an important lesson from Elijah. He taught us the prayer of faith. Let's get right to that scripture, which is found in James:

> *Is any one of you in trouble? He should pray. Is anyone happy? Let him sing songs of praise. Is any one of you sick? He should call the elders of the church to pray over him and anoint him with oil in the name of the Lord. And the prayer offered in faith will make the sick person well; the Lord will raise him up. If he has sinned, he will be forgiven. Therefore confess your sins to each other and pray for each other so that you may be healed. The prayer of a righteous man is powerful and effective. Elijah was a man just like us. He prayed earnestly that it would not rain, and it did not rain on the land for three and a half years. Again he prayed, and the heavens gave rain, and the earth produced its crops.*
> *(James 5:13–18 NIV)*

What a great testimony. What a great looking flower this one is. The color is tomato red. It's a ruffled flower with some olive coloring and is very interesting. Its 5–inch blossom tops a 24–inch stem. It looks nice in the garden.

Amazing Grace

God's grace is amazing, isn't it? Trying to find just the right scripture for this flower was very interesting. It was like preparing for a Sunday Bible school class. I really like the verses found in the book of Romans that teach about righteousness through faith. Let's look at them now:

> *This righteousness from God comes through faith in Jesus Christ to all who believe. There is no difference, for all have sinned and fall short of the glory of God, and are justified freely by his grace through the redemption that came by Christ Jesus.*
>   *(Romans 3:22–24 NIV)*

This "Amazing Grace" flower is a re-bloomer just like Christ's grace is to us. Its color is a creamy yellow. Its 26–inch tall stem has a 5–inch blossom. It's a nice plant to have as an early flowering bloomer in your garden.

Jericho

We all know of the battle of Jericho, of the song of Jericho ("and the walls came tumbling down"), and the Jericho march. It's one of those wonderful Bible stories taught to us in Sunday school. It's a scripture that teaches the power of faith!

> *By faith the walls of Jericho fell, after the people had marched around them for seven days.*
> *(Hebrews 11:30 NIV)*

This is another beauty. The colors are a pale gold with a red eyezone. It's bright and cheery. It has a 5–inch blossom on top of a 24–inch stem.

$\mathcal{C}\mathscr{S}$

Habakkuk

This is one of my favorite books in the Bible. I like it because of its great teaching of the Lord answering Habakkuk's complaints. Habakkuk 2:2–3 have always been special to me. Let's review the first part of Habakkuk's prayer from the third chapter:

> *A prayer of Habakkuk the prophet. On shigionoth.*
> *Lord, I have heard of your fame; I stand in awe of*
> *your deeds, O Lord. Renew them in our day, in our*
> *time make them known; in wrath remember mercy.*
> *(Habakkuk 3:1–2 NIV)*

This is a very special daylily. It is grayish lavender with a unique eyezone consisting of many bands of dark blue and purple that seem to blend into each other. It has a deep green throat. The stem is 22 inches tall with a big 6–inch blossom.

Ivory Gates

Well now, we have all heard of the pearly gates of heaven. There are, in fact, pearly gates in heaven, as described in the following scriptures. What I could not find is any reference to ivory gates. So let's assume that the flower "Ivory Gates" is referring to the color of ivory, and that with a little imagination we could see them as "ivory":

> *The twelve gates were twelve pearls, each gate made of a single pearl. The great street of the city was of pure gold, like transparent glass.*
> *(Revelation 21:21 NIV)*

This is another one of those repeat bloomers that gives you twice the beauty. As you would expect, the blossom is an ivory-cream color. Its 6–inch blossom sits on top of a 28–inch stem. It's a nice plant to repeat twice each year.

Glory Calls

What do you think the call of glory will be like? I think it will be a powerful call of many angels. As I looked through the Bible searching for the scripture to reflect this daylily's name, I came upon a wonderful part of Revelation that I think resembles a glory call:

> *Then I looked and heard the voice of many angels, numbering thousands upon thousands, and ten thousand times ten thousand. They encircled the throne and the living creatures and the elders. In a loud voice they sang: "Worthy is the Lamb, who was slain, to receive power and wealth and wisdom and strength and honor and glory and praise!"*
> *(Revelation 5:11–12 NIV)*

This is one of those rare double daylilies. It's a pink-colored 4–inch blossom. Its double makes up for the small bloom size.

True Glory

Now this verse is an easy one to select once you have reviewed all the verses referring to "glory." It's a great one—let's read it now:

> **When the Son of Man comes in his glory, and all the angels with him, he will sit on his throne in heavenly glory.**
>
> *(Matthew 25:31 NIV)*

This is a gold-colored flower just like the gold you will see in heaven. Its six-inch blossom re-blooms, giving you a twice-a-year preview of heaven. It is 26 inches tall. It will look nice in your garden.

Praise of Wisdom

In what part of the Bible do you think the most powerful scripture of the "praise of wisdom" is found? It's difficult to select one that is the most meaningful; however, I have identified one that to me is very powerful. As you would imagine, I found it in the book of Revelation. Let's read it now:

> *All the angels were standing around the throne and around the elders and the four living creatures. They fell down on their faces before the throne and worshiped God, saying: "Amen! Praise and glory and wisdom and thanks and honor and power and strength be to our God for ever and ever. Amen!"*
> *(Revelation 7:11–12 NIV)*

This is a beauty with some special "blessings." It is a violet-rose blend—one of the few daylilies with that coloring. It is also special because it is fragrant and is a repeat bloomer. With all of that in one plant, it's a must for your garden. It has a 6–inch blossom on a 20–inch stem. This one is nice—really nice.

He Touched Me

The book of Daniel is very interesting, especially with the scriptures that tell of Daniel's interpretation of the vision. In the eighth chapter, Daniel says the words "he touched me." Let's look at those words right now:

> *As he came near the place where I was standing, I was terrified and fell prostrate. "Son of man," he said to me, "understand that the vision concerns the time of the end." While he was speaking to me, I was in a deep sleep, with my face to the ground. Then he touched me and raised me to my feet.*
> *(Daniel 8:17–18 NIV)*

This is a beautiful porcelain-pink daylily. It looks great in a garden, especially when it is mixed in with some pink peonies that bloom so well in the spring. Try it with some "Angel Cheeks" peonies.

Realms of Glory

The heavenly realms that our Father gave us are found in the book of Ephesians in the first chapter. Here Paul writes to the saints in Ephesus about the spiritual blessings in Christ:

> *Praise be to the God and Father of our Lord Jesus Christ, who has blessed us in the heavenly realms with every spiritual blessing in Christ. For he chose us in him before the creation of the world to be holy and blameless in his sight.*
>
> *(Ephesians 1:3–4 NIV)*

This is an award-winning daylily (Honorable Mention in 1980) of the American Hemerocallis Society. It's a deep cherry-red color with a big six-inch blossom. It is a very early bloomer that sits on top of a 24–inch stem. It's a nice bright red color. Put it next to a white one—wow!

Judah

Judah was one of Jacob's sons. In Genesis 49, Jacob blesses his sons. He said, "Gather around so I can tell you what will happen to you in the days to come." Let's read the words he had for Judah:

Judah, your brothers will praise you; your hand will be on the neck of your enemies; your father's sons will bow down to you. You are a lion's cub, O Judah; you return from the prey, my son. Like a lion he crouches and lies down, like a lioness-who dares to rouse him? The scepter will not depart from Judah, nor the ruler's staff from between his feet, until he comes to whom it belongs and the obedience of the nations is his. He will tether his donkey to a vine, his colt to the choicest branch; he will wash his garments in wine, his robes in the blood of grapes. His eyes will be darker than wine, his teeth whiter than milk.

(Genesis 49:8–12 NIV)

This is a perfectly round, deep gold flower with some cinnamon brushing. It grows to be about 26 inches tall. This is a really nice bloomer.

Blessed Trinity

In the Bible you will not find a direct reference to the "Father, Son, and Holy Spirit." As I read through the Bible looking for scriptures that would be appropriate for this daylily, I was drawn to the verses in Luke where Jesus sent out the seventy-two. Let's read them now:

> *At that time Jesus, full of joy through the Holy Spirit, said, "I praise you, Father, Lord of heaven and earth, because you have hidden these things from the wise and learned, and revealed them to little children. Yes, Father, for this was your good pleasure. All things have been committed to me by my Father. No one knows who the Son is except the Father, and no one knows who the Father is except the Son and those to whom the Son chooses to reveal him."*
>
> *(Luke 10:21–22 NIV)*

The "Blessed Trinity" is one of those beautiful near-white daylilies. It has a nice 6–inch blossom on a 20–inch stem. Put it next to some of the red ones, such as the "Realms of Glory," for a nice treat.

❧

Heavenly Hope

I call this the "Hope of Glory"! We do not have to hope to go to heaven; we need to know Jesus as our Savior and then wait for the glory. Let's look at the verse that talks about hope:

> *To them God has chosen to make known among the Gentiles the glorious riches of this mystery, which is Christ in you, the hope of glory.*
> *(Colossians 1:27 NIV)*

We know that heaven will be beautiful—let me tell you that this daylily is also beautiful. Listen to the colors: very ruffled with peach-pink cream and a gold edge. Wow! That is a hint of heaven.

Golden Scroll

In Revelation we can find the scroll and the Lamb mentioned. Let's read the verses from the fifth chapter now to hear what the saints sang:

> *And they sang a new song: "You are worthy to take the scroll and to open its seals, because you were slain, and with your blood you purchased men for God from every tribe and language and people and nation. You have made them to be a kingdom and priests to serve our God, and they will reign on the earth."*
>
> *(Revelation 5:9–10 NIV)*

This bloom is a really nice tangerine color. It's one of those special daylilies that is a repeat bloomer for twice the enjoyment, and is also fragrant. The 5–inch blossom is on top of a 19–inch stem.

Angel's Voice

I just cannot wait to hear those wonderful angel voices singing praise and worship songs in heaven. Many verses in the Bible tell of the angels singing. Let's review one now:

> *Then I heard every creature in heaven and on earth and under the earth and on the sea, and all that is in them, singing: "To him who sits on the throne and to the Lamb be praise and honor and glory and power, for ever and ever!"*
> *(Revelation 5:13 NIV)*

Just like a pure angel, this is a beautiful, large (six-inch), well-formed, white daylily with a green throat. It's a wonderful plant for any garden.

Little Isaac

I did not know why the name of this daylily is "little" Isaac, rather than just "Isaac." As I researched this, however, I could see why someone would call him "little Isaac." In the Bible, Isaac was the promise from God, born when Abraham was one hundred and Sarah was ninety years old. Let's read that part of Genesis that tells the story:

> *God also said to Abraham, "As for Sarai your wife, you are no longer to call her Sarai; her name will be Sarah. I will bless her and will surely give you a son by her. I will bless her so that she will be the mother of nations; kings of peoples will come from her." Abraham fell facedown; he laughed and said to himself, "Will a son be born to a man a hundred years old? Will Sarah bear a child at the age of ninety?" And Abraham said to God, "If only Ishmael might live under your blessing!" Then God said, "Yes, but your wife Sarah will bear you a son, and you will call him Isaac. I will establish my covenant with him as an everlasting covenant for his descendants after him."*
> *(Genesis 17:15–19 NIV)*

This is a really pretty flower that would remind you of a little child. Listen to the colors: delightfully ruffled and frilled hot coral pink with deeper coral-pink knobs, edges, and fringes. Doesn't it sound great? An extra treat: it's a re-bloomer, with a 5–inch flower on top of a 26–inch stem.

Angelus Angel

As you read about angels, you will find out they have a hierarchy. Also, the term "angel" is derived from the Greek word *angelos,* which means "messenger." Many scriptures in the Bible refer to angels acting as messengers. Let's read one of my favorite "messenger" passages:

> **There the angel of the Lord appeared to him in flames of fire from within a bush. Moses saw that though the bush was on fire it did not burn up. So Moses thought, "I will go over and see this strange sight—why the bush does not burn up." When the Lord saw that he had gone over to look, God called to him from within the bush, "Moses! Moses!" And Moses said, "Here I am." "Do not come any closer," God said. "Take off your sandals, for the place where you are standing is holy ground." Then he said, "I am the God of your father, the God of Abraham, the God of Isaac and the God of Jacob."**
> **(Exodus 3:2–6 NIV)**

This angel is dressed in a cream-peach blend. It is a 24–inch stem with a nice 5–inch blossom.

Ezekiel

Ezekiel was a sixth century B.C. prophet. In the Old Testament we see that he saw visions of God. Let's read the first part of Ezekiel chapter one:

In the thirtieth year, in the fourth month on the fifth day, while I was among the exiles by the Kebar River, the heavens were opened and I saw visions of God. On the fifth of the month—it was the fifth year of the exile of King Jehoiachin—the word of the Lord came to Ezekiel the priest, the son of Buzi, by the Kebar River in the land of the Babylonians. There the hand of the Lord was upon him.
(Ezekiel 1:1–3 NIV)

This one is black. red, which is a very dark red. This would look really good with some nice white daylilies. It has a 28–inch blossom on top of a 28–inch stem. It's really striking.

Sunday Morning

We know that the Lord's Day is Sunday. One verse in the Bible refers to the Lord's Day, and that is in the book of Revelation. Let's read it now:

> *On the Lord's Day I was in the Spirit, and I heard behind me a loud voice like a trumpet, which said: "Write on a scroll what you see and send it to the seven churches: to Ephesus, Smyrna, Pergamum, Thyatira, Sardis, Philadelphia and Laodicea."*
> *(Revelation 1:10–11 NIV)*

This is a daylily that says "good morning." It's a six-inch round and ruffled brilliant lemon yellow that is always open flat from the throat. It is 24 inches tall.

Days of Heaven

How long are the days of heaven? Well, that is easy—they are forever. Let's look at a verse in Psalms that tells of establishing the Lord's line forever:

> *I will establish his line forever, his throne as long as the heavens endure.*
>
> *(Psalm 89:29 NIV)*

This is a 19–inch stem with a 5–inch blossom with a pinkish-lavender blend. It's special because it has an extended bloom time and is a repeat bloomer, two extras not found in many daylilies.

Timeless Fire

This name sure sounds like hell to me! There are a few verses in the Bible that talk of hell, but for this particular daylily, I think the very direct verse found in the book of Matthew is the most suitable:

> *If your hand or your foot causes you to sin, cut it off and throw it away. It is better for you to enter life maimed or crippled than to have two hands or two feet and be thrown into eternal fire.*
> *(Matthew 18:8 NIV)*

This is a deep red (like hot coal!) and is a repeat bloomer (like forever) and has a fragrance (no comment). It is 18 inches tall with a 5–inch blossom.

Grand Amen

What does "amen" mean? If you look up the word in a Bible dictionary, you will find out that it means, "so be it." That is kind of a matter-of-fact way of saying, "that's just how it is." I searched the Bible until I found a verse that I feel says just that. I found it in the book of John:

Jesus said, "You believe because I told you I saw you under the fig tree. You shall see greater things than that." He then added, "I tell you the truth, you shall see heaven open, and the angels of God ascending and descending on the Son of Man."
(John 1:50–51 NIV)

This is a fragrant 25–inch-tall flower. Each blossom on this plant is a very pretty 6–inch orange color. It's a grand daylily for a "Grand Amen."

Enchanting Blessing

I do not like the word "enchanting" when talking about the Lord's book. As I reviewed the Bible looking for a verse that would go well with this daylily's name, I came across an interesting blessing. Let's read it now:

> *Then I heard a voice from heaven say, "Write: Blessed are the dead who die in the Lord from now on." "Yes," says the Spirit, "they will rest from their labor, for their deeds will follow them."*
> *(Revelation 14:13 NIV)*

This is another repeat bloomer to give you a double treat. As a matter of act, as I write this page, I am able to look out of my den window and see the first bloom of the year. This is a very nice 6–inch pink blossom with a green throat and is 18 inches tall.

Divine Guidance

Zechariah 9:8 has the best scripture about having a divine guidance. Let's get right to it:

> **But I will defend my house against marauding forces. Never again will an oppressor overrun my people, for now I am keeping watch.**
> **(Zechariah 9:8 NIV)**

This is another nice pink daylily. It is 18 inches tall and has a 6–inch pink blossom. Try mixing those pinks with some white ones and get a great daylily show..

I Believe

I think this has to do with faith. Without faith you certainly could not believe in anything. As I looked through the Bible to find a verse that has to do with faith, I came across chapter 11 of Mark where Jesus told the disciples about faith. Let's read it now:

"Have faith in God," Jesus answered. "I tell you the truth, if anyone says to this mountain, 'Go, throw yourself into the sea,' and does not doubt in his heart but believes that what he says will happen, it will be done for him. Therefore I tell you, whatever you ask for in prayer, believe that you have received it, and it will be yours. And when you stand praying, if you hold anything against anyone, forgive him, so that your Father in heaven may forgive you your sins."
(Mark 11:22–25 NIV)

This is an evergreen daylily with a blossom that remains open for 16 hours each day. It is an appealing 5–inch light lavender blend with a green throat and stands 17 inches tall.

❦

New Testament

We know that this is the second part of the Bible and has 27 books. It includes the four Gospels. The books are:

Matthew, Mark, Luke, John, Acts, Romans, 1 Corinthians, 2 Corinthians, Galatians, Ephesians, Philippians, Colossians, 1 Thessalonians, 2 Thessalonians, 1 Timothy, 2 Timothy, Titus, Philemon, Hebrews, James, 1 Peter, 2 Peter, 1 John, 2 John, 3 John, Jude, and Revelation.

This is a pink-colored daylily with a six-inch blossom. It is a repeat bloomer that is 18 inches tall.

Song of Solomon

I think that the Song of Solomon is about love! As I looked through the Bible for the scripture to use for this daylily, I came across these verses in the third chapter of the Song of Songs:

All night long on my bed I looked for the one my heart loves; I looked for him but did not find him.
I will get up now and go about the city, through its streets and squares;
I will search for the one my heart loves.
So I looked for him but did not find him.
The watchmen found me as they made their rounds in the city.
"Have you seen the one my heart loves?"
Scarcely had I passed them when I found the one my heart loves.
I held him and would not let him go till I had brought him to my mother's house, to the room of the one who conceived me.
Daughters of Jerusalem, I charge you by the gazelles and by the does of the field:
Do not arouse or awaken love until it so desires.
(Song of Solomon 3:1–5 NIV)

This daylily has a big seven-inch flower that is a beautiful rose violet. It's great and tall, reaching 25 inches. What a wonderful flower for your loved one!.

Heavenly Crown

I went right to the book of Revelation to search for the best verse to match this daylily. I found just the right one in the fourteenth chapter. Let's read it now:

> *I looked, and there before me was a white cloud, and seated on the cloud was one "like a son of man" with a crown of gold on his head and a sharp sickle in his hand.*
>
> *(Revelation 14:14 NIV)*

This is a tall (28–inch) daylily with the coloring of a gold crown. It has a 5–inch flower that is a creamy yellow melon color. It looks like a crown. Nice.

❧

Jacob

This has always been a very interesting Bible study topic. We all know the story of Jacob and his brother Esau (the redhead with lots of hair), and how Jacob tricked his father Isaac into giving him Esau's blessing. It is interesting that this daylily is red (like Esau's hair)!

Let's read the scriptures that tell of the birthright's transfer:

> *So he went to him and kissed him. When Isaac caught the smell of his clothes, he blessed him and said, "Ah, the smell of my son is like the smell of a field that the Lord has blessed. May God give you of heaven's dew and of earth's richness—an abundance of grain and new wine. May nations serve you and peoples bow down to you. Be lord over your brothers, and may the sons of your mother bow down to you. May those who curse you be cursed and those who bless you be blessed."*
> *(Genesis 27:27–29 NIV)*

Just like Jacob, the namesake of this daylily, this flower is known as a vigorous one. It has a rich burgundy red blossom with a 6–inch flower on top of a 28–inch-tall stem. Very striking!

Song of Praise

It was very enjoyable to read through the Bible to find the verse that best describes the song of praise. There are many that would be so nice. I have chosen the excellent Psalm 113:

Hallelujah! O servants of Jehovah, praise his name. Blessed is his name forever and forever. Praise him from sunrise to sunset! For he is high above the nations; his glory is far greater than the heavens. Who can be compared with God enthroned on high? Far below him are the heavens and the earth; he stoops to look, and lifts the poor from the dirt and the hungry from the garbage dump, and sets them among princes! He gives children to the childless wife, so that she becomes a happy mother. Hallelujah! Praise the Lord.

(Psalm 113 TLB)

This is a beautiful lavender flower with a big 6_–inch blossom on top of a 21–inch stem. It's a nice flower, which again would look great with some whites.

Nicholas

As the word of God spread and the Christians grew in numbers, the time came to seek help from the disciples to minister to the people. Nicholas was one of those chosen.

In those days when the number of disciples was increasing, the Grecian Jews among them complained against the Hebraic Jews because their widows were being overlooked in the daily distribution of food. So the Twelve gathered all the disciples together and said, "It would not be right for us to neglect the ministry of the word of God in order to wait on tables. Brothers, choose seven men from among you who are known to be full of the Spirit and wisdom. We will turn this responsibility over to them and will give our attention to prayer and the ministry of the word." This proposal pleased the whole group. They chose Stephen, a man full of faith and of the Holy Spirit; also Philip, Procorus, Nicanor, Timon, Parmenas, and Nicolas from Antioch, a convert to Judaism. They presented these men to the apostles, who prayed and laid their hands on them.

(Acts 6:1–6 NIV)

This flower is one of the largest and showiest of all the daylilies. It has a seven-inch blossom with a beautiful gold self and a green throat. It sits on top of a 26–inch stem and is very impressive!

Rings of Glory

One interesting part of the Bible is where a prophecy came against Sidon. In that prophecy, a lesson was taught so that Sidon would see the glory of God. Then they would know that he was the Lord their God. Let's read that prophecy against Sidon:

> *The word of the LORD came to me: "Son of man, set your face against Sidon; prophesy against her and say: 'This is what the Sovereign LORD says: "I am against you, O Sidon, and I will gain glory within you. They will know that I am the LORD, when I inflict punishment on her and show myself holy within her. I will send a plague upon her and make blood flow in her streets. The slain will fall within her, with the sword against her on every side. Then they will know that I am the LORD."'"*
> *(Ezekiel 28:20–23 NIV)*

This is a lavender-pink blossom with a wire edge of light yellow. It has a chalky yellow watermark and a bright yellow throat with a green heart. The petals are very wide on the 4–inch flower. It stands 21 inches high.

❀

Holy Spirit

We use the name of the Holy Spirit very often today as we pray and give praise to the Lord. The words "Holy Spirit," however, are not mentioned in the Bible very often. My favorite verse for it is in Luke's writing of the upcoming birth of the Christ child:

> *The angel answered, "The Holy Spirit will come upon you, and the power of the Most High will over-shadow you. So the holy one to be born will be called the Son of God."*
>
> *(Luke 1:35 NIV)*

This is another great repeat bloomer with a 6–inch flower. It has a nice cream self and a green throat. It's an early bloomer and is 20 inches tall.

Printed in the United States
785500002B

9 781591 603399